THE KINDERGARTEN TOOLKIT FOR PARENTS

Published by Kristen Sutich, LLC, 4810 Point Fosdick
Dr NW, Suite 430, Gig Harbor WA 98335

Cover Design by Yale Winter

Artistic Design by Bryce Winter

Illustrations by Shida Davis

ISBN-13: 978-1502527448
ISBN-10: 1502527448

This book is dedicated to all kindergarten
students. May your first year of school be
full of learning, excitement and new adventures.

"It's what you do that counts."

Violet Richardson Ward

Contents

Introduction.. 1

Chapter 1: Is My Child Ready for Kindergarten?.... 4

Chapter 2: Schedules and Routines 10

Chapter 3: Backpack and Supplies......................... 21

Chapter 4: First Day of School 27

Chapter 5: Adapting to All Day School.................... 37

Chapter 6: How Will I Know What My Child
Does All Day?.. 43

Chapter 7: School Work and Homework 47

Chapter 8: Food at School 56

Chapter 9: Safety at School 61

Chapter 10: The Big Yellow School Bus 69

Chapter 11: Bullying Issues and How to
Get Along 74

Chapter 12: Unique Circumstances........................ 78

Conclusion 84

Acknowledgements... 86

About the Author 87

Learn More With Kristen 89

"Kindergarten is that first big step in growing up. Embrace this new opportunity with your child."

Kristen Sutich

Introduction

When I was a kindergarten teacher I noticed how stressed parents were during the "meet the teacher" event, and on the first day of school. Some had tremendous anxiety over the thought, "my baby is leaving me." Most parents were not staying in the present moment, instead they were thinking about what could happen in the future. They were stressing themselves over things that hadn't even happened yet. Without meaning to, some of this stress and worry transferred to their children. This is why I decided to write this book. No parent or student needs to suffer this much before the first day of kindergarten! It is not necessary. Almost everyone is a little nervous, and that's a normal reaction to anything new. I was a little nervous and excited meeting a new group of students and parents for the first time each year.

This is why I enjoy coaching. I am able to support and guide parents through a smooth transitional period in their lives. In my 15 years of teaching, I observed many parents who could have used the support of a coach. To find out more about me and my coaching, please visit: www.kristensutich.com, or contact me at: kristen@kristensutich.com.

I trust you will enjoy this book and find it helpful by providing you with some simple and easy ways to help transition you and your child into the world of k-12 education. This book will provide tips to help make your life easier while adjusting to this new phase of life for you and your child. This book also makes a great gift for people you care about. Best wishes to you and may your kindergartner have a wonderful first year of school!

"What if life is a school? What if you haven't failed, but simply completed that lesson? What if your future is pulling you towards your destiny?"

Aurora Winter

Chapter 1

Is My Child Ready for Kindergarten?

This is a popular question among parents. Every child appears to develop at a different rate and pace. I'm definitely an advocate for preschool. In my experience, this makes a huge difference when entering kindergarten. If every child had at least one year of preschool, they would be much more prepared and ready for kindergarten academically, socially and emotionally as well. I also feel this would help the students feel more comfortable about beginning school.

States may differ slightly in their rules/laws for beginning school. In Washington, if a child turns five at least the day before school starts, they can enroll in kindergarten. In my district if a student wasn't quite yet five, but would be turning five soon, they could take an assessment at the district office to determine whether they could begin the current school year or not.

Anxious parents often described their child's abilities and then asked me if their child was ready for kindergarten. Parents seemed stressed and overwhelmed as to whether to send their child to kindergarten, or wait another year. The back and forth debate that went on inside parents' heads had to be exhausting and emotionally draining. I would love to coach parents through this time period, and help make the experience less stressful and more enjoyable for everyone involved.

In my experience, students that had at least one year of preschool, and knew some of the basics had an easier transition into all day and even half day kindergarten. Those that didn't sometimes struggled more, at least at the beginning of the school year. Since parents know their own children best, they'll want to look at their child's social and emotional well being. If they are very immature for their age, or have a difficult time getting along with their peers, then spending one more year in preschool may be a good choice. These are the areas where the parent knows their child.

When I was a kindergarten teacher, I had quite a range of students in my classes. I would typically have 1–3 students entering who could already read and could count way beyond 100 if you let them, some students that knew almost all letters and sounds and perhaps could count to 50, students that knew some letters and sounds and perhaps could count up to 20 or so, and then usually a few who did not know any letters and sounds other than the ones in their own name and most likely could count up to 10.

Once in a blue moon I would have someone who knew 0 letters and sounds, couldn't tell me any letters in their name nor attempt to write their own name and counting past three was a huge challenge. This was usually rare, but academically this child was not ready. The advantage of a year of preschool for this student, could result in a lot less struggle for her.

Something parents were often surprised by, was when I would share screening results such as: "Your child knew 15 letters and 8 sounds." They would usually say something like, "They know the whole alphabet. I've heard them name all of the letters." Yes, but was that in random order? Or, were they singing their ABC's? When screening most teachers are going to ask your child to look at a sheet of paper with letters in random order including upper and lower case, and ask your child to name as many letters as they can. Same with letter sounds. This child has a good start. There may be some struggle in the beginning, but with parent support at home, they will be able to handle it.

If your child attended preschool, ask the preschool teacher for her opinion as to whether she feels your child is ready for kindergarten.

If you decide to wait, be okay with that. Your child can attend preschool for another year and perhaps take advantage of some play groups, or join story hour and programs at your local library or community center. Museums often have educational events that you and your child can check out. Look for those catering to children, especially at children's museums.

If you decide to enroll your child, ask your child's teacher for suggestions on ways to help support your child's learning at home. Get involved and take an interest in what she is learning in school.

Tips: Is My Child Ready For Kindergarten?

- If your child meets the minimum age requirement for entering kindergarten in your state, province or country, they may go.

- If your child knows a minimum of 10 letters and 8 letter sounds in random order and can count to at least 10 on their own, they will have a nice start.

- Give some thought to your child's social skills and emotional well being.

- If your child has been in a preschool program, ask your child's preschool teacher for her opinion and feedback.

- If you decide to wait a year for kindergarten, enroll your child into a preschool program, especially if they have not yet been to preschool.

- Read with your child each day.

- Look for opportunities for your child to socialize with other children her age.

- Checkout www.starfall.com which is a free website with a lot of fun ways for children to learn letters, sounds, words and beginning reading skills.

"Obstacles don't have to stop you. If you run into a wall, don't turn around and give up. Figure out how to climb it, go through it, or work around it."

Michael Jordan

Chapter 2

Schedules and Routines

Be prepared: Reduce anxiety by registering your child as soon as you can, get all of your paperwork turned in, get a supply list and attend any orientations or open houses offered.

Attend the "Meet the teacher" event if your school offers one. This way you and your child get to meet your child's teacher, see the classroom and meet other students and parents that will also be a part of that classroom. Your child may be a little nervous at that meeting, and many will be excited. That's okay, I was always a little nervous myself, and I was the teacher! After all, I was meeting almost a whole new group of students and parents, with maybe a few known families to me. It was always an exciting time though. A new adventure about to begin!

This is usually a pretty informal event. Most teachers will save their presentations for "parent night" or "curriculum night," a few weeks down the road. This is usually a meet and greet event where students can look around the room, find their cubby and table sort of thing. I recommend using this opportunity to show your child where the closest restroom is located to your child's classroom. If possible, walk your child around the building a bit. Stop by and say "hi" to the school librarian, the P.E. teacher in the gym and the school music teacher. Your child will be visiting these teachers most likely 1-3 times a week depending on your school's schedule. It's a good idea for your child to learn where the office is from the beginning. Let's say you and your child head out to your car one winter morning only to discover that your car has a dead battery. (It happens.) Well, your child will be late for school and will need to check in at the office first before heading to her classroom. The reason for checking in at the office is that your child's teacher may have already taken attendance for the day, and has marked your child absent. The office needs to know that she is now present at school. The office is probably where the principal has her office, as well as where the school nurse is located. If not, those would be good places to explore as well. If your school has a lunchroom, your child may be interested in seeing where this is located. This is a good time to show your child where the closest restroom to the lunchroom is located as well. Don't worry if you don't have time to point out all of these areas to your child. Your child will learn the school layout rather quickly once school begins. The students will see a lot of these areas and visit many daily, so they will learn where they are located very fast.

Make sure your child's teacher and the school office knows how your child will be going home each day. This is crucial. Will your child ride the bus home from school? Will someone pick your child up by car using the parent drop off/pick up car queue? Will they walk home? Discuss with your child how they will be going home each day. It's important for your child to know this information, but in case they forget, your child's teacher will have the schedule. Send a note on the first day with your child's going home schedule, and send a note anytime there is a change. Perhaps every Monday and Wednesday your child will ride the bus home, and every Tuesday, Thursday and Friday mom or dad will use the parent pick up car queue. Make sure the note is clear about the specifics especially if it's different depending on the day of the week. If you share custody of your child with your former spouse or partner, make sure the school office has both parents'

information on file and the specific going home schedule for your child. This information is something your
child's teacher will need in order to put your child in
the correct line or spot at the end of the school day.

Read and Save

Read all newsletters and notes that the teacher hands out, as well as news from the school within 24 hours if possible. This is important to follow all year long. You don't want to miss out on "special guest day" because you forgot to check your child's backpack with the info, or tossed it in the recycle bin before reading it. Make a folder for information you want to keep during the year. Do this for each child in school. Put the folder somewhere safe so you can easily refer back to it. Don't keep your child's special papers and projects in there; maintain a separate box or drawer for those items that you want to save. Also, have a special place for school library books. Trust me! This will save you time and anxiety so you're not scrambling every Wednesday morning before the bus arrives to find that library book so your child will be allowed to check out another book that day.

Routine

Set up a routine for your child even if you've never really had one before. The sooner you do, the easier everything will fall into place. Stick with the plan even if it's hard at first. Schedule: Homework or practice time for your child, the time you read with your child every night, the time lights are out and the time your child gets up in the morning. Make sure you add some time in the morning for your child to eat a healthy breakfast before school. It's important to have a "real" bedtime in place, and this may have to change when your child comes home exhausted. (More on this topic later.)

If your child has food allergies, I recommend you only have them eat food they bring from home. Whether it's your child with food allergies, or some-one else's child in the class, it is a good idea to ask the teacher/principal what the policy is for peanut and tree nut allergies. Does your child's school have a separate table in the lunchroom for those eating a peanut butter sandwich for lunch, peanuts of some kind or other tree nuts? If so, you can help explain this to your child and why it's so important to follow these rules. It may seem like an inconvenience for you and your child, but think of the child with the allergies, and how dangerous it can be for them. You can work out something for class birthday treats with the teacher if you are allowed to bring in treats. (Here's an idea for children with food allergies: The child's parents provide a box or bag of safe snacks that their child can have when other students are having a birthday treat. These can be kept in the classroom.)

Decide what you would like your child to do with her backpack (filled with papers) each day when she comes home. Are you going to go through the backpack every day? I don't recommend you wait until 9:00pm. What if your lovely angel forgot to tell you about a homework page due the next day? If so, have them place their pack in a specific area everyday when they get home. If you want them to be responsible for part of this, have a basket, file tray or specific shelf that you want them to lay their folder (if all papers are truly inside) or papers that the teacher/school sent home. This includes homework, newsletters, updates, flyers, info from PTA, etc. Remember the library book rule as well. Have your child get out their lunchbox which may very well be messy inside and full of partially eaten food and empty wrappers or containers.

Praise your child each day for following this routine, make corrections when necessary. If your child needs more motivation, perhaps a star chart would help. They receive a star on the chart for each day they follow their routine without being asked. (Some children respond to star charts, and some don't. It's worth a try.) Pretty soon you won't have to double check their backpack or wonder if there is something else inside.

Be happy and excited for your child. Many students are so excited to go to school! They can't wait for homework even! Reciprocate their enthusiasm. They will look at you to see how you are reacting to the situation. If you aren't sure about your child's teacher, they may not be sure about her either. I don't recommend you verbalize any negative thoughts or fears within ear shot of them. This just sets your child up for doubt. It's okay for you to feel various emotions as your child goes to school, but be excited and joyful for your child. They will never have a first day of kindergarten again.

Tips: Schedules

- Register your child for kindergarten as soon as possible.

- Attend any orientations at your child's school.

- Decide how your child is going to get home each day after school and give this information to the school office and your child's teacher by the first day.

- Create some files for teacher/school newsletters and important papers.

- Choose a safe spot in the house for school and/or classroom library books lent to your child.

- Choose a spot for your child's backpack and for school papers if your child is going to help you unpack them.

Tips: Routines

- Set up a routine for checking your child's back-pack.

- Decide your child's lunch routine. Will they buy lunch, or will you pack a lunch? Choose containers and food items for packed lunches.

- Have your child sample some possible lunch options during the summer months. Note which ones your child enjoyed.

- If your child has food allergies, discuss this with your child's teacher before school begins. Make a plan if necessary.

- Set up a schedule for: Homework, reading with your child, lights out, getting up and eating breakfast.

- If your bedtime routine will change, begin at least one month prior to the start of kindergarten, sooner if possible.

"When you are inspired by some great purpose, some extraordinary project, all your thoughts break their bonds; your mind transcends limitations, your consciousness expands in every direction, and you find yourself in a new, great and wonderful world."

Patanjali

Chapter 3

Backpack and Supplies

Your child's school supply list may include a large backpack. As a parent, you may be wondering "why in the world does my five year old need a large backpack?" You would be amazed at how little can actually fit inside a small pack. As a kindergarten teacher, my rule was at the end of the day when you pack up, nothing should be in your hands when you head to the bus or pick up lines. "Everything going home needs to be in your backpack." Believe me; I had many students try to get away with this. Even at the end of the school year, someone would try to carry their homework, coat, or lunchbox. If the students are holding something, there is much more potential for them to lose something on the way out the door, on the bus, standing outside at the pick up line or walking home. This prevented extra phone calls on the day pictures or report cards went home. This would be the alternative: "Why didn't my child get her pictures today?" "My daughter brought her report card home, how come my son didn't? Didn't you send them home today?" Yep, I sure did!

I wanted everything in their backpack. So, by the time they put their papers in their folder, their lunchbox, library book on some days, some students keep an extra clean pair of undies and pants in their backpacks for those "oops" days, and when it's warm out they don't want to wear their coat/sweatshirt and so that ends up in there as well, and Presto! Their backpack is full! I've actually asked parents at the beginning of the year if I could give their child a larger backpack to use instead of their small one. Some days they will have larger things to take home or bring to school such as sharing, science projects, show and tell items or big art projects that they get to take home.

A lot of teachers like to collect the school supplies and use them as a community within the classroom. This is most likely to occur if your child's classroom has tables instead of desks. With tables there really isn't a place for each child to keep their own separate supplies. It is much easier to have some kind of supply caddy on each table with all of the needed supplies offered to the whole table. I never liked to keep glue at the table, especially at the beginning of the school year. (Can you guess why?) It was just too tempting for those little darlings, so I would keep a separate bin with just glue. When the students needed it, they could go get it and then put it back when finished with that activity or project. (This was sometimes the case with scissors depending on the students that year. Yes, did you ever have a child that liked cutting her own hair? Oh yes, it happens in class too. Turn your back for one minute, and someone has just given themselves a $1.97 new hairstyle. At least it wasn't their tablemate, well, most of the time it wasn't. One year the kindergarten teacher next door had a student cut his own eyelashes! Yes, really, his eyelashes. Yes, that's a fun phone call home. Not!

If your child's classroom has desks, then it's likely that each child will keep their own supplies in their desk for the year. That's when it's wise to label your child's supplies with their name. While I'm on the subject of labeling, please, please. Do everyone a favor, and label all of your child's sweatshirts, jackets, coats and lunchboxes. You wouldn't believe the unclaimed clothing and items that sit in the school lost and found each year. Many items are never claimed! As a teacher, I often wondered how parents didn't realize their child had been missing all of their coats for months. My friend who teaches 5th grade looked in the lockers for her upcoming students right before school started and was shocked to see three coats left in a locker from the previous year! If no one claimed these items, we'd donate them to the Goodwill, or some other organization that could really benefit from children's clothing. At least they went to a good cause. If you want your items back, please label with your child's first and last name.

Tips: Backpack and Supplies

- Buy a backpack large enough to hold all important items.

- Make a date to go school supply shopping with your child.

- Label supply items if requested. Label all personal belonging that will accompany your child to school such as coats and lunchboxes.

- Discourage your child from bringing personal items to school such as toys, stuffed animals, jewelry that your child prefers to play with and not just wear, etc. Save these items for special days such as show and tell. These items can be distracting, take up space in your child's backpack and could be misplaced.

"The truly successful person inspires others to do more than they have thought possible for themselves."

Denis Waitley

Chapter 4

First Day of School
Part 1

This is such an exciting day for a new kindergarten student! For many five and six year olds, this is the day they have been thinking about and waiting for. If they have older siblings, cousins or friends with older siblings, they have most likely heard all kinds of interesting facts and opinions about kindergarten and school. Finally it is their turn!

The first day of school is also a very exciting day in the lives of parents. It is a day that some parents have dreaded. For others, they are in disbelief as to how their newborn has grown up and is ready for their first day of kindergarten already. For some, it is truly a relief. Their child is in school now, and the family no longer has to pay for child care. They know their child is in a safe and happy place.

Many students will be nervous on the first day. This is completely normal and natural. The same is true for how parents are feeling. It is how you react to these feelings in front of your child. Your child will look to see how you are reacting. It's okay to be nervous and even a little emotional, but remember, there will never be another first day of kindergarten for your child. So embrace this as a milestone. Be happy and excited. Some great things to say are: "I can't wait to hear all about your first day when you get home from school today." "I look forward to hearing about your two favorite parts of kindergarten today." "Do you think you'll be able to tell me the names of three students in your class?" If your child hasn't already dropped off their school supplies, you could help them put those items away, or help your child follow the instructions from the teacher. Many classrooms have a community arrangement for sharing their supplies due to sitting at tables instead of individual desks. The teacher may ask students to sort their supplies into bins that are set up around the classroom. If your child hasn't located their cubbie or locker and their place to sit, this would be something to do right away on that first day.

Find out ahead of time the protocol for that first day. Does the teacher invite parents to stay for the very beginning? Will there be a group tour? Does the entire school attend an assembly? Does the teacher prefer you drop your child off and then leave? If you know what to expect ahead of time you can be prepared and help prepare your child as well. Maybe you want to take a picture of your child standing next to their locker or cubbie or sitting at their table? This may be the start of a fun first day of school picture tradition.

Find out if your child's school has a special breakfast or meet and greet sponsored by the PTA the first day for parents/guardians of kindergarten students. If so, this may be a nice way to meet some new people who are experiencing the same thing you are. Take advantage of these opportunities if you can. Getting involved in your child's school is a fun way to stay informed about what is happening at school, as well as getting to know other parents and making new connections.

It is possible that the kindergarten students may begin school on a different day from the rest of the grade levels. Some schools have a system of easing their youngest members into school. There may be "getting to know you" conferences that take place the first few days of school. Some kindergarten teachers may like to do a couple basic assessments with the new students prior to the first day. This is a great opportunity to see what skills students already have.

For students who are attending half day, the day will go by quickly. Perhaps it would be fun to plan a special lunch at home to welcome your child back from school. For those attending all day, it may make things easier for students to bring their own lunch on the first day. That way they can see and learn how the lunchroom works before buying their lunch at school if that is an option for them. If the students eat in their classroom, then they can learn that routine as well.

Don't be surprised if your child comes home from the first day tired. Be enthused about their day and ask a few questions that require more than a yes or no answer. However, in your excitement try not to bombard them with too many questions all at once. They may like some down time to process their day. The first few days of school are full of learning about rules and procedures which requires a lot of listening power, and may not be quite as exciting for some students. Try not to be discouraged if your child doesn't have as much to say as you had hoped, or if they are feeling a bit disappointed that they haven't gotten to "play with everything" yet! I remember vividly how all my students wanted to do the first few days was play with all of the fun things found in the classroom. It can be difficult for a five year old to understand that it can't be a free for all, especially in a classroom with 20 or more students. Discussions about how to keep everyone safe, why we don't run in the classroom and how to take turns are very important. If there are only three student computers, then there may be a rotating schedule which means it will take a week or so before everyone has a turn. For many students, kindergarten is very different from preschool or daycare. They learn quickly that this is the real deal. They are in school to learn, and it isn't about playing all day. This can be challenging for some, but most students really begin to embrace the idea very quickly. They begin to understand the daily routine and look forward to it. They know when to expect "down" time and look forward to their recess breaks and choice time if this is something their class does.

First Day of School
Part 2

What about those students who don't want to go to kindergarten and are not excited for the first day?

First, start by asking yourself a question. Do you think your child is ready for kindergarten? Is there some reason why he/she may not be ready?

Next, find out why your child thinks they don't want to go. If they don't have older siblings or older friends they may have no clue what kindergarten is. Start by explaining that kindergarten is something almost everyone does. It is the first step in the school process after preschool. Touring the school your child will be attending, attending orientations and "meet the teacher" events can help show your child what kindergarten and school is all about. Reassure your child that it's normal and natural for her to feel nervous or even scared. This is completely new. If you think that first day is going to be a challenge, discuss this with your child's teacher. Set up a plan ahead of time for that first day. Ask the teacher what would be the easiest and smoothest transition when it's time to say goodbye.

I always found it much easier if the parents left the room/school as quickly as possible if their child was having a hard time. The longer the parents stay, the more difficult it seems to become. Even if your child is upset and looks like they are miserable, it's amazing how quickly most of them calm down after 5–10 minutes. Even if it takes longer than that, they are now part of the classroom community with their teacher and classmates. Your child will likely be distracted by what the teacher is saying, by watching the other students or engaging in the first activity of the day, and will soon forget that they were sad to say goodbye to their mom and dad. You can feel good about sticking to your plan even though it may have been hard on you. It won't get any easier if you prolong the "goodbye," or allow your child to talk you into staying in the classroom. When this happens, it continues to be hard the next day and the following until the cycle is broken. It also makes it difficult on the other students, since their parents have already left. Sometimes they start to question or wonder, "Maybe my mom should have stayed longer." Or, "why didn't my dad stay, if Katie's dad got to stay?" The classroom structure wasn't designed to include every parent along with the students. The sooner everyone gets set on the routine, the easier it is for everyone involved including the students, the parents and the teacher.

If your child is hesitant that first day, remain positive and continue to follow the routine that you've discussed with your child and her teacher about the first day. Be as flexible as you can and follow the plan for the day. If you are really worried, you can always call the school later on, and ask how your child is doing. Your child's teacher will be very busy, but the office can relay the message, or she will check her messages as soon as she can. Rest assured, if the teacher or school really needs to get in touch with you, they will. This is why it is very important to make sure all of your phone numbers are correct and up to date. If you get a new phone number, make sure the school and your child's teacher has it right away.

After the first day, if you have an older child attending the same school, you may consider having that child walk your kindergartner to their line or classroom. I did have several students that were walked to their line at the beginning of the year by an older sibling. From my experience it worked quite well. For some reason it was a smoother transition to say goodbye to their brother or sister, than to their parents. If your child doesn't have an older sibling, perhaps there is a neighbor child that your child trusts that attends the same school or, another kindergartner in the neighborhood and the two of them could walk to their lines or classrooms together once they enter the school building.

Tips: First Day of School

- Begin your daily routine.

- Follow first day instructions from your child's teacher and/or school.

- Pack a lunch for your child for less stress on the first day.

- Begin special memories! Take a first day of school picture.

- Make sure you, your child and your child's teacher knows how your child is getting home that first day and then for the rest of the year.

- Show enthusiasm along with your child. Share in their excitement and reassure if necessary.

"Excellence is to do a common thing in an uncommon way."

Booker T. Washington

Chapter 5

Adapting to All Day School

Don't be surprised if your child comes home wiped out that first week of school. For most students, this is probably a pretty big change in their daily routine. As a teacher, I always thought September was a tough month! It is all new, and everyone is trying so hard and learning routines. It is an extremely important month for your child to be present in school. The whole class really begins to bond with one another. The teacher and students begin to feel like a family. Your child is at school for an average of 6.5 hours a day with his/her teacher and other students. It is quite natural for everyone in a classroom to start feeling like a family of sorts. Once you get past September or the first month, things start to flow into everyday patterns and it's not quite so exhausting. This is where parents may need to adjust bed times, routines, meals, and extracurricular activities. Your child may need more sleep now. They will be tired from a full day of learning. With that being said, you may need to start looking at your child's diet needs a bit more as well. See Chapter 8, Food at School.

This is where that solid home routine can really support you, your child, and your whole family. It may be difficult at first, but it will pay off. The sooner you start that routine, the sooner you can start benefitting from it. This includes the times your child goes to bed, gets up, meals, clothes set out and lunches/snacks packed the night before, backpacks by the door ready to go with homework and any notes for the teacher inside, what your child will do when they get home from school, when is homework time, dinner etc. A lot of students benefit from a little down time when they first get home from school. A healthy snack and a quick share about the day would be a good start. You have to look at your own schedule to determine what comes next. Are you headed out the door to an activity? Are you in for the night? Most students do best getting their homework done right away before it gets any later into the evening. It's likely that the homework will become more challenging for your child, and it will take longer for them to finish it, the later it gets.

Routine Checklist

Clothes set out the night before

Lunches/snacks packed the night before

Backpacks by the door ready to go with homework and any notes for the teacher included

Read with your child

Bedtime

Time your child gets up

What's for breakfast?

What does your child do when they return home from school?

Homework

Dinner

Bath/shower

Tips: Adapting to All Day School

- Check your routines. Are they in place? Tweak if needed.

- Check the homework.

- Bedtime? Would a half hour earlier help?

- Make sure your child is eating a healthy breakfast each morning.

- If your family is very busy, you may want to have a chart with all activities listed for everyone in the family M-F. Include weekends if it helps you out.

"The classroom community will resemble a family. It's amazing how quickly the students and teacher bond with one another."

Kristen Sutich

Chapter 6

How Will I Know What My Child Does All Day?

This is a common question from parents. They worry they won't know what their child is learning and doing all day since they aren't there. That's the growing up part about kindergarten.

"My son won't tell me anything about his day," complains a parent. "My daughter only talks about P.E.

and lunch," says another parent. As a teacher, I heard these comments often. Here is what I suggest: Number one, give it some time. Everything is new at the beginning of the year, and can be somewhat overwhelming for your child. It is a lot to take in. Some children are big talkers, while others are not. You know your child best, so that will give you some indication as to whether you think you'll hear a lot or not. Think about your day. Do you want to relive the whole day as soon as you get home from work? When your child gets home from school, they may need some down time. They may not feel like reliving the whole experience over again just for mom and dad's benefit. Start slowly with something you think they really enjoy. Maybe it is recess or P.E. Perhaps they just made a new friend, and they love sharing about this new person in their life. Your child may be ready to share more at dinner time. Ask about their favorite part of the day. Ask and take an interest in specific subjects or themes that may be occurring. Perhaps your child is learning about the life cycle of an apple tree or how pumpkins grow. In my class we often studied spiders in the fall.

If your child loves science, then focus in on these areas. If your child loves reading, ask if her teacher read a favorite book today. What subject or theme is the class or her reading group focusing on?

Are there any field trips or special assemblies taking place soon? I always took my kindergarten class to the pumpkin patch in October. This was surely a hot topic of discussion at home. Most of the students were very excited to attend the field trip and ride a school bus. Those topics will likely get them talking and sharing. Have your child participate at home in the responsibilities. Once you've signed the parent permission form, ask your child to place it in her folder and then right into their backpack. (It's okay, you can watch as they do this so you know it was done.) Ask your child what they would like to have in their sack lunch for the field trip, and have them help you put it together the night before.

Tips: How Will I Know What My Child Does All Day?

- Be patient with your child.

- Give your child some down time when they first get home from school.

- Ask your child about their favorite part of the day.

- Be engaged in what your child is currently involved in at school and in their classroom.

- Have your child help you with planning or preparation of special events or activities. (Example: Help plan and pack their sack lunch for an upcoming field trip.)

Chapter 7

School Work and Homework

Overall, students in kindergarten are working hard with their letters and sounds. They are learning how a string of letters with the sounds that the letters make, create a word. They are learning that some letters are silent, while others have more than one sound. They are working on memorizing sight words. Sight words are common words that appear often in beginning reading books. These words are often words that cannot be sounded out, but best memorized. When the student has a bank of sight words memorized, it is easier to read a beginning book. They start to see those basic words pop up all the time, and it helps the reading feel smoother and there's more of a flow to the reading. Some examples of beginning sight words are: the, a, in, it, you, can, what, here, are, I'm.

Students are working on recognizing and counting up to 100 and how to combine and take apart numbers up to ten. Identifying and describing shapes, and even create and solve basic word problems involving numbers up to ten.

Students in the United States typically need to be five years of age by the time their school begins in the fall. When I taught, I had quite a range with ages. I've had students who turned five two days before school began all the way to students who had been six for several months before the first day of kindergarten. Due to a district waiver, I even had a couple students who were still four when school started and then soon turned five. With the range of ages, also comes a huge range in abilities. Some students may enter kindergarten already reading, while others may enter with no letter and sound knowledge. Teachers will work hard to meet the individual needs of the students.

There may be different reading groups created within the classroom so students can learn at their level. It doesn't work well to have students trying to sound out words, when they don't know the letter sounds yet.

If they can work hard on learning those letter sounds, it will be much easier for them to start reading words a few months down the road. Students who are already reading beginning books, may be assigned specific books for independent reading. They may sit down with their teacher later that day, or the next to explain the characters in the story and what took place. At this point those students are starting to focus on their story comprehension.

Ask your child's teacher if you have specific questions or concerns about what your child is learning in school.

Homework

Homework for kindergarten students helps to reinforce what the students are learning in the classroom, and teaches students about responsibility. It also gives parents a chance to see what their child is working on in class that week. My personal opinion is that young children don't require very much homework. If they are attending all day kindergarten, they are working hard all day, and don't need a large amount of work in the evening. Spending 15–20 minutes a day at home reviewing letters and sounds for those students without this knowledge, is an appropriate homework assignment. Once they can recognize all letters and letter sounds in random order without any hesitation, they could spend the 15–20 minutes a day at home working on sight words. Also, reading every day is very beneficial. Being read to daily, and then having your child read to you once they know their letters, sounds and a few sight words is an excellent habit to get into as soon as possible. I noticed the students who did this daily practice at home, made faster progress than those that did not read at home on a regular basis. It also starts to build a positive routine at home.

Paper homework helps your child build responsibility. Some students may need some assistance with this task, while others will quickly become quite independent with their homework. Even for those that want to do their homework completely on their own, it doesn't hurt to take a look and check it over with them before they pack it away in their backpack. They take the paper home, complete it with their best writing, coloring and return it by the due date to their teacher. For some students this takes some practice, and will be a very important skill to have as they get older. Remembering to check their backpack each morning when they enter the classroom, get out any notes, lunch money and homework and place it in the proper spot is huge. By practicing this in kindergarten, it will become routine by the time they enter first grade. I know how frustrating it is for teachers and parents when a student has their homework, book report or special project complete, but forgets to turn it in! As students get older, points may be taken away or grades may drop because an assignment or project was not turned in on time. By supporting your kindergartner with this positive habit now, will save lots of heartache down the road.

I often told my parents not to stress over the homework. If you're having a really busy evening, or your child is cranky and tired, don't push the homework. It's not worth it at that point. Try not to make this the usual routine, or the homework habit won't stick. It is easy to let the homework slide one week, and then forget to get back on track the next. There are ways to fit it into your schedule. Have your child read their list of sight words or sight word flashcards aloud to you or have them read one of their beginning reading books to you while you are making dinner in the kitchen, or cleaning up after dinner. Pack your child's sight word cards in your purse or leave an extra set in the car for those moments when you are waiting to pick up or drop someone off at soccer practice, ballet lessons, piano lessons and so forth. Use those extra minutes in your day to help your child get their practice or homework completed for the day. You could have your child be responsible for packing their book, lists or cards to help them take some ownership in the process. After all, it is their homework, not yours. Students would often say, "My mom forgot to put my homework in my backpack." My standard response was something like, "Oh, you forgot to put your homework in your backpack today.

"Remember to find your homework and put it in your backpack when you get home today."

A lot of families have more time on the weekends, so one suggestion is to dedicate some time to homework practice on those days especially if you missed a day or two during the week. If you have more time, and are feeling less stressed on Saturday, then dedicate some time for homework then. It might be fun to let your child create a Homework Chart with you. Each day they complete their homework or practice, they can put a check, sticker or star by that day. Have your child count up all the days they completed their homework after a couple weeks or at the end of the month. They will feel very proud of themselves, and a routine will have been established as well.

Tips: School Work

- Ask your child what they are learning in school and how they feel about it.

- Take an interest in what your child shares with you. If they really want to work on a science project for the school science fair, offer your encouragement and support.

- Support your child with extra help at home if needed.

- Ask your child's teacher how your child is doing in a particular subject if you are concerned or suspect your child is having more difficulty than expected. Don't wait until the next scheduled conference.

Tips: Homework

- Ask your child each day if they have homework or something to practice.

- Check your child's backpack, especially at the beginning of the year in case your child forgets about their homework.

- Find a good homework space in your house for your child, and supervise their efforts.

- Offer encouragement while your child completes their homework, and praise once they have finished.

- Encourage your child to put their homework in their backpack as soon as it's completed.

"Always do right. This will gratify some and astonish the rest."

Mark Twain

Chapter 8

Food at School

If your child is a picky eater, most likely you will be sending them with a lunch daily. Some students like to buy milk every day even if they bring their lunch from home. If your school offers this, it's something to consider. If your child is going to buy lunch daily at school or often, it is easiest on everyone to prepay for many lunches ahead of time. Each school will have their own system, but I suspect a lot of schools have a system to pay for your child's lunches online now. If not, sending a check for 25 lunches will keep your child up to date. This way your child won't have to handle cash, or worry that there won't be enough left in their lunch account. It is hard for the younger students to keep track of how many lunch credits they have left, and they likely will forget to tell you when they are down to one.

If your child's school has the online system, you can probably go into your account and see how many lunches your child has left. I suspect most parents are not aware what happens when students don't have enough lunch money in their accounts. I can't speak for every school district, but this is what took place in the district I worked for. A student was allowed to charge up to two lunches once their account had a zero balance. After those two charges were issued and the student still didn't have lunch money, the lunch person would not allow them to buy a school lunch. Instead they were given a peanut butter sandwich and plain milk for lunch that day. If the child had peanut allergies, they were given a cheese sandwich. I recently saw something regarding this on the news more than once which lead me to believe most people didn't know how this issue was handled. I know how it worked at my school because I saw it take place often. Most young students and even some older ones forget to tell their parents that they need more lunch money. That is why I often encouraged parents of my students to check their child's lunch accounts online, or if I knew their child was running low, I sent them an email letting them know. This is not something a lot of teachers will do because it's time consuming, but I know parents appreciated the information. If you qualify for free lunches, your child will never run out and parents won't have to keep track of anything. You may have to fill out paperwork each school year in order to qualify for free lunches, so be sure to check at your child's school at the beginning of each school year.

Encourage your child to eat a good portion of their lunch during their lunch break, and not use it only as a social time. The afternoons can be quite long. If you know there's something your child doesn't like or won't eat, save it for someone else in the family. Time and time again I watched young students throw away perfectly good food items simply because they said they didn't like it. I'd always say, "Tell your mom you don't like apples." The waste drove me crazy! Sometimes just having a cute or colorful container to hold part of their lunch may entice them to eat it. Perhaps you could put a very small treat in their lunch and tell your child they can eat it after they eat their healthier choices. I was quite amazed at how many kindergarten students followed this plan later on in the school year. It became a routine. They knew they could eat their treat after their sandwich and fruit. (It didn't hurt that I was often standing nearby at the beginning of their lunch reminding them all to eat their healthy choices first.)

Some schools ask students to bring a small healthy snack from home to eat sometime during the day. I encouraged parents to add an additional item to their child's lunch that could be their snack. It's also a good idea to share with your child where and what their snack is. This worked well for those students that brought their lunch daily or almost daily. It is helpful to explain to your child that we don't share snacks or any food with other students at school. While sharing is a nice thing to do, some students have food allergies and this could cause a serious problem. It also lessens the amount of germs being spread by handling each other's food. Here are some snack suggestions that I would propose to my kindergarten parents.

Pretzels, raisins, cheese and crackers, fruit, veggies, yogurt, are just some examples. Nuts are great if your school/classroom isn't "tree nut and peanut free."

Depending on what time your child eats their snack may determine what type of snack you send. If it is something that needs refrigeration, it may only work if your child eats their snack in the morning. It may work to send the snack with a small ice pack included. A lot of parents would do this.

Tips: Food at School

- Discuss whether your child will bring their lunch from home, or buy at school most days.

- Make sure you understand any food allergy rules and policies that your child's school may have.

- Find out if you can pay online for your child's school lunches and set up an account if possible, or find out if your family qualifies for the free lunch program.

- Have a plan to make sure your child doesn't run out of lunch money, especially if you can't check their account every week.

- Encourage your child to eat most of their lunch during their lunch break and not just socialize.

- Discuss some favorite and healthy lunch and snack options that your child enjoys and will eat.

- Check in with your child at least once a month to see if they are still enjoying the food items you originally discussed together as good lunch and snack options.

Chapter 9

Safety at School

afety at school has always been a concern for parents. For specific rules and regulations at your child's school, please check with your local school district and the school itself for safety procedures and policies. Some procedures may vary depending on what school district you are in. Your child's classroom teacher can share school safety procedures, and what the students will be instructed to do in the classroom if there is an emergency.

Everyday safety aspects: Most teachers have a policy that students don't leave the classroom without asking for permission first. This is important, especially with young children. The teacher won't know where your child is if they wander out the door. The teacher can't leave the other students alone in the classroom to go search for the "wandering student." I certainly experienced a handful of wanderers in my teaching career. Usually they weren't far away. Sometimes they were out in the hallway or peeking into the gym to see what the students were doing in P.E. that day. Sometimes they would go to the restroom. I would gently remind them that they need to let me know before leaving the room so I know where they are at all times. If you know your child is a wanderer, or has a difficult time following these types of rules, be sure to share this with the classroom teacher prior to the first day of school. It is much easier for the teacher to be prepared with this knowledge, than be surprised by it. Some basic routines or procedures can be set into place if the teacher knows this could be a challenge for a particular student.

Drills at school: Most schools are required to have a certain amount of drills throughout the school year. For specifics, check with your child's school on what kinds of drills are taught and conducted and how often they take place.

Fire Drill: One of the most common drills is the fire drill. You may remember doing this when you were in school. For kindergarten students this may be very new to them. If they attended preschool they may have experienced some drills. Being in a larger building with grades K-5, K-6 or even a building with students K-12, the whole drill experience will be different than what your child experienced in preschool or daycare. It will be helpful to talk to your child about this at home as well, in order to help reinforce what your child is being taught at school. I always encouraged students to go home and share their knowledge of what to do during a fire drill with their parents. I also suggested that it would be a good time to discuss and create a plan for what to do if they have a fire in their home. What is the exit plan? Backup plan? Where does the family meet once outside? If you haven't discussed this with your family, it would be a good idea. Hopefully you never have to use your plan, but if there is a fire emergency, everyone in the family will know what to do. At school the fire alarm is usually very loud. This in itself can be scary to young children, or for those with special needs. I tried to prepare my students and explain that it has to be loud so everyone hears it right away and takes action immediately. The most important thing I explained to the students is that we stop everything we are doing no matter what, and get to the door as quickly as we can without running. We then exit the building quietly using the closest door to our classroom. The teacher may be required to take a walkie talkie with them or perhaps even an emergency bag that is found near the door.

Once outside I always emphasized that the students' job was to stand in line quietly. Each teacher has to count their students and make sure everyone is present, and it is much easier to do this without them wiggling all over and being noisy! A tricky part for young students is if they aren't with their class when a drill occurs. I would prep my students ahead of time about what to do if they are in the hallway or in the bathroom at the time. I taught them to exit the closest outside door and find an adult. They were instructed to tell the adult who their teacher was and they would help them get to where our class was, or have them join another class until they could meet up with their own class. I emphasized that it was very important that they didn't stay in the bathroom or try to go back to the classroom. They immediately needed to get outside. Once students experienced one drill and understood why we had to practice this, it became routine and much easier for everyone involved.

Earthquake Drills: These are a little more technical. Again each school district may have their own procedures for dealing with an earthquake so please check with your child's school for specifics. At the school I worked at, we were told to drop and cover. This is what I instructed my students to do. If the students were close to a table or desk, they were to get under one, use one hand to cover the back of their head/neck area, and to hold onto a table or desk leg with the other. If they were walking down the hallway, or in a place without a table or desk, they were instructed to drop away from windows and cover their head/neck area with both hands. Once we were given a signal or the ground had completely stopped shaking, everyone would line up at the door and exit the building using the closest and safest exit outside. Students were accounted for, similar to a fire drill.

Lockdown Drills: This drill was used if there was an intruder in the building or if something had occurred in the community near the school. (I never experienced a situation where there was an actual intruder in the building. We did lock down one time when our local police were searching for someone in the area that was under investigation.)

This drill involved the students getting down onto the floor and being very quiet. The teacher or staff member would lock the classroom door, turn off the lights, close any open windows and pull blinds over any exposed windows. I had a walkie talkie, so I would turn this on low in order to hear any instructions from our principal or other staff members. Some lockdowns only required that we close our blinds and lock our doors, but we could continue with our teaching and learning. The tricky part about this drill was if students were out of the classroom at the time. This required explaining how important it was that they get to a classroom with an adult who could lock their door. No hiding in the bathroom or hallways. Teaching them to knock loudly on the closest classroom door and to tell the teacher who they were was the challenge. That's why we would practice these situations. If we ever had an emergency, I wanted the students to know what to do. That was what I reinforced each time after we had a drill of any kind and a student asked why we had to do that.

Depending on where you live, there may be other drills necessary. Drills regarding what to do during a tornado, hurricane or tsunami may be necessary in some parts of the United States as well as in other countries.

Tips: Safety

- Ask for information on school and classroom safety standards and procedures if you are unsure of them.

- Discuss common drills and procedures with your child in an easy going manner.

- Address any concerns or fears your child brings up, and reassure him or her the reasons for practice drills and knowledge of what to do in specific situations.

- Address any of your fears or concerns away from your child and get further clarification from your child's teacher or school principal.

"All dreams can come true, if we have the courage to pursue them."

Walt Disney

Chapter 10

The Big Yellow School Bus

Some students will ride a school bus to and from school. Some parents feel they do not want their child riding a school bus in kindergarten, while others embrace the idea and love not having to drive them to and from school every day.

Bus drivers have bus rules just like teachers have classroom rules. Most bus drivers will go over the rules on the first day or throughout the first week of school. Some schools have a bus coordinator, or someone in charge of bus issues. That person may go over bus rules with the children who are going to be riding the bus during the school year. There likely will be something going home pertaining to the bus rules as well. If you have questions about the bus, I would ask to speak to the bus coordinator or someone at school that can answer those questions. Most parents with young students will stand at the bus stop each morning and watch their child get on, and then do the same at the end of the day when they return. Ask the school what the policies are regarding being at the bus stop. Do you have to be waiting? Will the bus driver let your child get off if you aren't standing there? It is always good to have a backup plan in case you are running late one day. Can a neighbor meet the bus? If your child is allowed to get off without a parent there, where do you want your child to go if you're not there one day?

If your child has been issued a bus tag by the school with their name and the bus stop address, please make sure they wear it, or that it is attached to their backpack. It may be required for kindergartners to have a tag on their backpack all year long. If this is the case, please make a new one or ask the school for a new one if your child loses their tag or it gets worn. There may be days when your child has a substitute bus driver, and they want to check which stop your child gets off at.

If there is a problem with the bus or bus driver, talk to someone at your child's school right away to help get the issue resolved.

Help support the bus driver. He has a bus full of students to transport back and forth each day. It's going to make his job much easier if the students are not overly loud on the bus, stay seated at all times and follow the other bus rules. The rules are there for safety reasons. If your child rides the school bus, go over the basic rules with your child, and help them understand why they are important.

The school I worked for had the kindergarten students load the bus first at the end of the day. This was really helpful. I always encouraged my kindergarten students to sit toward the front of the bus, near the bus driver, especially at the beginning of the school year. Some schools or bus drivers may insist on this. Personally, I agree with this. I think it is helpful.

Tips: School Bus

- If your child will be riding the school bus, make sure the school knows this and that both you and the school know which bus and bus stop your child will be using.

- Help your child remember to wear their bus tag, or make sure the correct information is listed in or on their backpack.

- For young students it's always a good idea to have your child's information pinned to the inside of their backpack all year long. (Child's name, bus stop address, parent phone numbers) Do not put your child's home address for safety reasons.

- If you have any concerns with the bus driver or other students on the bus, address these issues right away with someone at your child's school.

- Discuss bus rules with your child prior to the first day of riding.

- Have a backup plan for those days when you are stuck in traffic and can't get to the bus stop on time. (Do you have a neighbor that can be at your child's stop? Can you have someone pick your child up that day instead of having them ride the bus home? Make sure to inform the school of any change of plans as early as possible, and have the school inform your child's teacher and your child of the changes prior to the end of the day.)

"Teaching kids to count is fine, but teaching them what counts is best."

Bob Talbert

Chapter 11

Bullying Issues and How to Get Along

Bullying is a tough topic. It is heard about in the news and media frequently, and although I believe there have always been bullies, now society speaks about them more and does not tolerate their behavior.

I recommend you contact your child's teacher and principal right away if you are concerned with another student bullying your child. It may very well be true, that your child's teacher is not aware of a particular situation, especially if something has taken place at recess. Teachers and principals go through classroom and school rules at the beginning of the school year with periodic refreshers now and then depending on the grade level. As a kindergarten teacher, I felt like I discussed almost daily some rule or character trait with my students. It may have been brought up if something happened during the day, or the topic had been an ongoing issue during the week. Our school focused a lot of attention on showing kindness and compassion to others, so we often talked about what that meant. We would have mini problem-solving lessons. "What could you do if someone says something you don't like?" "What could you do if you're playing on the big toy at recess and someone won't leave you alone?" We would discuss, and sometimes list on the board or on a sheet of paper helpful ideas and suggestions, versus choices that were not helpful, or that would not solve the problem.

I highly recommend having discussions at home with your child about how to handle different situations with other children. Kindergarten is going to be a huge year for learning about how to get along well with others. For some students, the focus may be more on how to speak up for themselves and to not be afraid to go ask a teacher or staff member for help with a situation. For others, the focus may be on how to not be so bossy or controlling with friends and classmates. Learning how to give others a chance to be first in line or make the choice of what and where to play that day.

Tips: Bullying Issues and How to Get Along With Other Students

- Contact your child's teacher and/or principal at first signs of concern with bullying.

- Begin a comfortable routine of talking to your child about bullying and what they can do if another student is bothering them.

- Try role playing with your child regarding possible bullying situations.

- New situations for your child will appear throughout the school year. Use them as an opportunity for learning and growing.

"The most important single ingredient in the formula of success is knowing how to get along with people."

Theodore Roosevelt

Chapter 12

Unique Circumstances

There may very well be years when your child's class has unique circumstances. It may be that one of your child's classmates loses a parent or sibling during the school year. There could be a student in your child's class that has a serious illness or physical disability that requires extra help and attention. It is quite possible that some of your child's classmates may only have one parent in their life, or perhaps are being raised by their grandparents. There may also be a child in class that has two dads or two moms. Depending on the circumstance, your child will likely bring up the situation at some point and have some questions regarding it.

Kindergarten is a huge time for learning. One theme that I brought up with my students throughout the school year, was respect for others. As the teacher, I couldn't make classmates be friends, nor would I want to force a friendship, but I always expected everyone to be respectful of each other. This included how they spoke to one another, how they treated one another, and how they responded during learning opportunities. If someone didn't solve a math problem correctly, a student could certainly point it out during our class discussion. Another could come up and demonstrate the correct way, or another way of solving the math problem, or show how they would solve it. What we didn't do, was focus on why they did it "wrong" or criticize them for solving the problem incorrectly.

Being prepared with some basic knowledge and thoughts as to how to address these different scenarios with your child, will help to make the discussion smoother when and if it ever occurs. One of the best things you can do if you are the parent in a unique situation, is make arrangements to speak to your child's teacher before school begins. (An open house event or meet the teacher night is not the most appropriate time since there will be many families attending, and all will want the teacher's attention for at least a couple minutes. You will want a more private time to share your concerns.) Share your concerns with her at an appropriate time, and if necessary come up with a plan to help your child and family in the most productive way. During kindergarten registration you could mention that you would like to speak with whoever is going to be your child's teacher regarding your circumstance. The school may not know for a few more months down the road who your child's teacher will be, especially if registration is very early, such as in the month of March. Some of the paperwork that you fill out may include an area for your concerns. You could share your concerns in that section so that the school principal and kindergarten teachers are aware of your situation right from the beginning.

I did have a student one year that lost a younger sibling. I could see the family grieving, and wanted to support my student and her family. The outpouring of care and compassion from the other families in the class was well received. It was so nice to see that we could support this family during their time of need.

I also had a student one year with two dads. I witnessed such an outpouring of love from this family, and I could easily tell the student's parents wanted her to have a successful start to school, as any family would. Their main concern was whether their daughter would be treated like all of the other students. Would she be teased by the other students because she had two dads? The dads were also concerned that they may be shunned by other parents, or perhaps even by their child's teacher and principal because they were gay.

While I can't speak for every teacher or parent, I certainly hope that all teachers and parents would be respectful of a student's personal situation. As a teacher I noticed that students, and especially young students were curious about things, and once they were given some information, they were often satisfied and moved on to other thoughts and ideas. Most just wanted to know the basics, and that was enough. Often times adults are not as easily satisfied, and can spend time and energy involving themselves in someone else's business.

I once had a student that was missing a few of his fingers. That same year I had another student that spoke in a whisper voice due to some vocal cord polyps. On the first day of school an opportunity presented itself when both students shared their situation. All of the students in the classroom saw and heard from these two students, and it wasn't a big deal. The students learned that Brandon could still write and do just about everything they could do with all of their fingers. They also learned that there would be times when they may have to ask Kelly to repeat herself when she couldn't be heard the first time. Just like that, everything was out in the open, and we moved on to other topics.

It was a great opportunity to discuss how people are different, and that we all come with special and unique qualities.

Tips: Unique Circumstances

- Share any unique circumstances with your child's teacher prior to the first day of school.

- Make an appointment to speak to your child's teacher to ensure privacy.

- Talk with your child about being respectful to their classmates and their unique circumstances.

- Think ahead to how you might start a conversation with your child regarding various topics or answer your child's questions.

- If gossip presents itself in your circle, ask yourself, "does this concern me and is it any of my business?"

"Tenderness and kindness are not signs of weakness and despair, but manifestations of strength and resolutions."

Kahlil Gibran

Conclusion

I trust you have found this tip book to be a helpful tool and resource for you as a parent, and as a gift to give others. My intention is to provide simple tips presented in a fun way that will allow you to begin the school process with your child, minus the stress and anxiety. By following these guidelines and suggestions, you can begin the school year on a peaceful note, and continue this same existence throughout the school year. Laying a solid foundation now, can set you and your child up for success.

It is my great joy to not only be a teacher, author and speaker, but to be a coach and support system for parents. For even more support for yourself and your family, please contact Kristen at: www.kristensutich. com or email her at: kristen@kristensutich.com.

Best wishes for a happy and successful school year.

"Go confidently in the direction of your dreams. Live the life you have imagined."

Henry David Thoreau

Acknowledgements

Thank you to my husband, Dan Sutich for all of his love and support over the last 17 years.

I'd like to thank my family and friends for being on my side and offering support and positive words. Special thanks to: Mom, Tom, Aimee, Tom and Nita.

Thank you to JoAnn Fuller, AKA Grandma Jo, for being the best and most faithful grandparent volunteer I ever had.

I'm grateful to all of my friends and former co-workers at Browns Point Elementary. I treasure my years of working there with all of you.

Thank you to all of my coach friends at Grief Coach Academy. It has been a pleasure getting to know you and I appreciate all of the peer practicing, triads and masterminds.

Thank you to my mentor Aurora Winter, for your heartfelt support and encouragement with this book, as well as with my grief coach training.

Thank you to Babette Zschiegner for all of your support, encouragement and friendship during our monthly coaching calls and masterminds.

About the Author

Kristen Sutich is a former elementary school teacher and certified From HeartBreak to Happiness® Coach who studied with Aurora Winter, founder of Grief Coach Academy. Kristen understands the challenges and stress parents face when their children are entering kindergarten, starting a new school or entering a new phase in education. She now coaches parents through an easy and smooth transition resulting in peace, confidence and joy. She was born and raised in the Pacific Northwest where she continues to live today with her husband Dan. Disneyland remains one of her "happiest places" on Earth. She would like to help you become happier too!

To find out how Kristen can personally support you, please visit: www.kristensutich.com or email her at: kristen@kristensutich.com.

"I loved witnessing the growth and change that took place with my students each year. It was a magical time, and I was happy to be a part of it."

Kristen Sutich

Learn More With Kristen

It is my passion to support and help parents of school aged children transition smoothly through this time of change. Coaching is the best way for me to support you, and I look forward to speaking with you. If you would like more support, please send me an email.

Send to: coach@kristensutich.com. Please include:

1. Your name and phone number
2. Best time to call
3. Time zone
4. Your children's ages

As an experienced teacher of 15 years and the author of The Kindergarten Toolkit for Parents, I would like to share more with you by speaking at your school or club. Please contact me using the above email or go to: www.kristensutich.com for more information.

Made in the USA
San Bernardino, CA
24 December 2014